はしがき

　本書『Active　Practical Reading 基本編』は，大学入学共通テスト，英検®，GTEC®に対応した速読問題集です。近年のリーディングの問題では，大意把握や情報検索といった速読の力がますます重要になってきています。そのため本書では，与えられた英文から必要な情報を短時間で見つけ出す「スキャニング（探し読み）」の技能を，"Practice makes perfect!"（習うより慣れよ。）を実践しながら身につけることができるように構成しました。各レッスンで用意した実用的で多様な英文と設問を通して，本書がみなさんの大学入試に向けた英語学習に役立つことを期待していま~~す~~

【本書の構成と利用法】

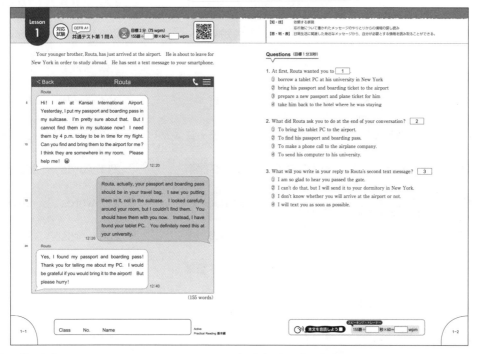

●左ページ：本文

・各試験の英文形式に対応した本文です。

・本書ではレッスンが進むにつれて，1分あたりに読むべき語数（wpm）がだんだん多くなるように目標時間を設定しています。上部（⏱）の計算式を使って，読みの速度を算出してみましょう。

・二次元コードを読み取って，本文の音声をPCやスマートフォンから聞くことができます。（英文形式によって，一部の音声が収録されていないレッスンがあります。）

●右ページ：設問

・各試験の設問形式に対応した設問です。（設問数は異なります。）

・求められる「知識・技能」と「思考力・判断力・表現力」をページ上部（【知・技】【思・判・表】）に示しました。

・スピーキング・トレーナーを使って，本文の音読練習をすることができます。下部の計算式を使って，1分あたりに音読できた語数（wpm）を算出してみましょう。

CONTENTS

Lesson	対応試験		テキストタイプ	本文語数	目標 wpm	
1	共通テスト	第1問A	メッセージ	155 words	75 wpm	
2	英検®3級	第3部A	掲示	109 words	75 wpm	
3	GTEC®	パートB	説明文	98 words	75 wpm	
4	共通テスト	第1問A	メール	138 words	75 wpm	
5	共通テスト	第1問B	ウェブサイト	237 words	75 wpm	
6	英検®3級	第3部B	メール	200 words	78 wpm	
7	共通テスト	第1問B	告知記事	220 words	78 wpm	
8	共通テスト	第1問B	ポスター	237 words	82 wpm	
9	共通テスト	第2問A	レシピ	201 words	85 wpm	
10	共通テスト	第2問A	採点表+コメント	198 words	82 wpm	
11	共通テスト	第2問B	ブログ記事	211 words	85 wpm	
12	GTEC® 英検®準2級	パートC 第4部B	説明文	212 words	90 wpm	
13	共通テスト	第2問A	説明書	230 words	90 wpm	
14	共通テスト	第2問B	ネット記事	254 words	90 wpm	
15	英検®準2級	第4部A	メール	236 words	90 wpm	
16	共通テスト	第3問A	記事	261 words	95 wpm	
17	共通テスト	第3問A	ブログ記事	247 words	95 wpm	
18	GTEC® 英検®準2級	パートC 第4部B	説明文	239 words	100 wpm	
19	共通テスト	第3問B	雑誌記事	295 words	100 wpm	
20	GTEC® 英検®準2級	パートC 第4部B	説明文	285 words	100 wpm	
21	共通テスト	第3問B	記事	304 words	100 wpm	
22	共通テスト	第3問B	記事	305 words	100 wpm	

求められる資質・能力	
知識・技能	思考力・判断力・表現力
□依頼する表現／□忘れものについて書かれたメッセージのやりとりからの情報の探し読み	□日常生活に関連した身近なメッセージから，自分が必要とする情報を読み取ることができる。
□自然に関する表現／□バスツアーについて書かれた掲示からの情報の探し読み	□日常生活に関連した身近な掲示から，自分が必要とする情報を読み取ることができる。
□言語(学習)に関する表現／□英語学習について書かれた説明文からの情報の探し読み	□平易な英語で書かれたごく短い説明を読んで，概要を把握することができる。
□注文に関する表現／□注文後の対応について書かれたメールからの情報の探し読み	□日常生活に関連した身近なメールから，自分が必要とする情報を読み取ることができる。
□時間や条件を表す表現／□上映スケジュールについて書かれたウェブサイトからの情報の探し読み	□平易な表現が用いられている身近なウェブサイトから，自分が必要とする情報を読み取り，書き手の意図を把握することができる。
□依頼する表現・時間を表す表現／□空港での待ち合わせについてのメールのやりとりからの情報の探し読み	□平易な英語で書かれたごく短いメールのやりとりを読んで，概要を把握することができる。
□予定を表す表現／□イベント内容について書かれた告知記事からの情報の探し読み	□平易な表現が用いられている告知記事から，自分が必要とする情報を読み取り，書き手の意図を把握することができる。
□イベント内容について書かれたポスターからの情報の探し読み	□平易な表現が用いられているポスターから，自分が必要とする情報を読み取り，書き手の意図を把握することができる。
□料理方法や数量に関する表現／□料理方法が書かれたレシピからの情報の探し読み	□身の回りの事柄に関して平易な英語で書かれたごく短い説明を読んで，イラストを参考にしながら，概要や要点をとらえたり，推測したり，情報を事実と意見に整理することができる。
□評価する表現／□スピーチコンテストについての採点表と審査員のコメントからの情報の探し読み	□身の回りの事柄に関して平易な英語で書かれたごく短い説明を読んで，図表を参考にしながら，概要や要点をとらえたり，推測したり，情報を事実と意見に整理することができる。
□言語に関する表現／□第二言語習得について書かれたブログ記事からの情報の探し読み	□身近な話題に関して平易な英語で書かれた短い説明を読んで，概要や要点をとらえたり，推測したり，情報を事実と意見に整理することができる。
□時間的順序を表す表現／□ジェンダーについて書かれた説明文からの情報の探し読み	□身近な話題に関して平易な英語で書かれた短い説明を読んで，概要を把握することができる。
□組み立て方に関する表現／□組み立て方が書かれた説明書からの情報の探し読み	□身の回りの事柄に関して平易な英語で書かれたごく短い説明を読んで，イラストを参考にしながら，概要や要点をとらえたり，推測したり，情報を事実と意見に整理することができる。
□義務や禁止を表す表現／□ネット記事からの校則についての情報や，その意見内容に関する情報の探し読み	□身近な話題に関して平易な英語で書かれた短い説明を読んで，概要や要点をとらえたり，情報を事実と意見に整理することができる。
□依頼する表現／□職業に関するイベントについて書かれたメールからの情報の探し読み	□身近な話題に関して平易な英語で書かれた短いメールを読んで，概要を把握することができる。
□過去の出来事・経験を描写する表現／□夏祭りについて書かれた記事からの情報の探し読み	□平易な英語で書かれたごく短い物語を読んで，イラストを参考にしながら，概要を把握することができる。
□旅行や位置関係(場所)に関する表現／□旅行について書かれたブログ記事からの情報の探し読み	□平易な英語で書かれたごく短い物語を読んで，イラストを参考にしながら，概要を把握することができる。
□共通することを表す表現／□双子について書かれた説明文からの情報の探し読み	□平易な英語で書かれた短い説明を読んで，概要を把握することができる。
□食事作法に関する表現／□文化について書かれた雑誌記事からの情報の探し読み	□平易な英語で書かれた短い説明を読んで，概要を把握することができる。
□環境や旅行に関する表現／□エコツーリズムについて書かれた説明文からの情報の探し読み	□平易な英語で書かれた短い説明を読んで，概要を把握することができる。
□時や場所を表す表現／□音楽と技術発展について書かれた記事からの情報の探し読み	□平易な英語で書かれたごく短い物語を読んで，概要を把握することができる。
□長所や短所を表す表現／□決済手段について書かれた記事からの情報の探し読み	□平易な英語で書かれた短い説明を読んで，概要を把握することができる。

Lesson 1

対応試験

CEFR A1

共通テスト第1問A

目標2分 (75 wpm)
155語÷ □ 秒×60= □ wpm

Your younger brother, Routa, has just arrived at the airport.   He is about to leave for New York in order to study abroad.   He has sent a text message to your smartphone.

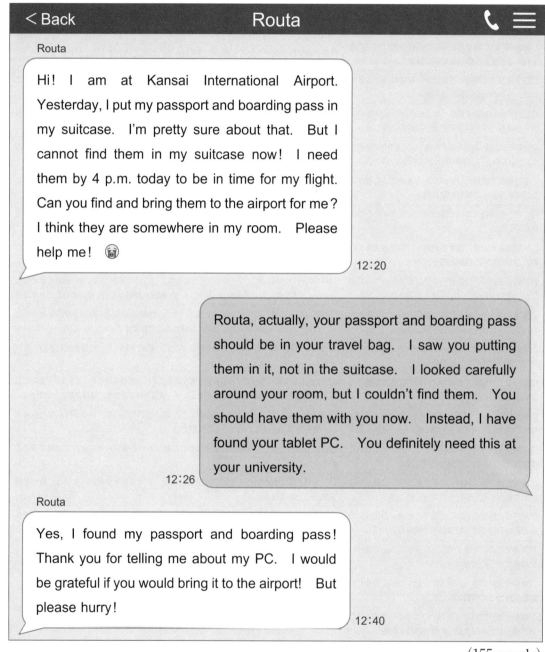

< Back　　　　　　　　　Routa

Routa

5　Hi! I am at Kansai International Airport. Yesterday, I put my passport and boarding pass in my suitcase.   I'm pretty sure about that.   But I cannot find them in my suitcase now!   I need them by 4 p.m. today to be in time for my flight. 10　Can you find and bring them to the airport for me? I think they are somewhere in my room.   Please help me!

12:20

Routa, actually, your passport and boarding pass should be in your travel bag.   I saw you putting them in it, not in the suitcase.   I looked carefully 15　around your room, but I couldn't find them.   You should have them with you now.   Instead, I have found your tablet PC.   You definitely need this at your university.

12:26

20　Routa

Yes, I found my passport and boarding pass! Thank you for telling me about my PC.   I would be grateful if you would bring it to the airport!   But please hurry!

12:40

(155 words)

Class　　No.　　Name

Active
Practical Reading 基本編

Questions（目標1分30秒）

1. At first, Routa wanted you to 　1　.
   ① borrow a tablet PC at his university in New York
   ② bring his passport and boarding ticket to the airport
   ③ prepare a new passport and plane ticket for him
   ④ take him back to the hotel where he was staying

2. What did Routa ask you to do at the end of your conversation? 　2　
   ① To bring his tablet PC to the airport.
   ② To find his passport and boarding pass.
   ③ To make a phone call to the airplane company.
   ④ To send his computer to his university.

3. What will you write in your reply to Routa's second text message? 　3　
   ① I am so glad to hear you passed the gate.
   ② I can't do that, but I will send it to your dormitory in New York.
   ③ I don't know whether you will arrive at the airport or not.
   ④ I will text you as soon as possible.

Lesson
2

 対応試験

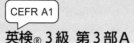 CEFR A1
英検® 3級 第3部A

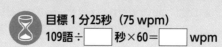 目標 1 分25秒 （75 wpm）
109語÷□秒×60＝□wpm

Bus Tour to See Amazing Animals!

Australia is famous for being a great place for watching unique animals! If you want to see them, please visit Daintree National Park. This park is home to some unusual animals, such as crocodiles, colorful wild birds, and Australian frogs.

5 Tour buses leave every 15 minutes from 9 a.m. to 5 p.m. You can buy a ticket at our information center. We are closed every Monday.

Ticket Prices
Adults: $20

Children 3 to 14: $10

10 Children under 3: free

If you are looking for accommodations near the park, please check our website below. You will find the best lodging for your trip.

www.amazinganimals.au

(109 words)

Class　　No.　　Name

Active
Practical Reading 基本編

【知・技】　自然に関する表現
　　　　　バスツアーについて書かれた掲示からの情報の探し読み
【思・判・表】　日常生活に関連した身近な掲示から，自分が必要とする情報を読み取ることができる。

Questions （目標1分30秒）

1. What is this notice about? ☐ 1 ☐
   ① An animal tour with a tour guide.
   ② An exhibition of animals of Australia.
   ③ Bus tours to see Australian animals.
   ④ Information about Australian animals.

2. People cannot get a tour bus ticket ☐ 2 ☐.
   ① at the information center
   ② from 9 a.m. to 5 p.m.
   ③ if they are under 3 years old
   ④ on Monday

3. The website will tell you ☐ 3 ☐.
   ① how to enjoy the night events in the park
   ② some information about places to stay
   ③ some information about ticket prices
   ④ where to buy a tour bus ticket

What is the best way to learn English as a foreign language? In Japan, all junior high school and high school students have to study English at school. It seems that the total time of all the English classes for six years at school is at most about 1,000 hours. However, some researchers say that learners need at least about 3,000 hours to learn
5 English. Therefore, one important thing in learning English is that you should use it as often as possible outside of school. As you spend more time using English, you will get better at it.

(98 words)

Class　　No.　　Name

【知・技】　言語(学習)に関する表現
　　　　　英語学習について書かれた説明文からの情報の探し読み
【思・判・表】　平易な英語で書かれたごく短い説明を読んで，概要を把握することができる。

3-2

Questions （目標 1 分30秒）

1. What is this passage mainly about? ☐ 1 ☐
   ① A good way to improve our English skills.
   ② The current situation of English education in Japan.
   ③ The reason why we should learn English.
   ④ The total time we need to master our native language.

2. How long do we need to learn English? ☐ 2 ☐
   ① At least about 1,000 hours.
   ② At least about 3,000 hours.
   ③ At most about 1,000 hours.
   ④ At most about 3,000 hours.

3. An important thing in learning English is ☐ 3 ☐.
   ① how long you stay in a foreign country
   ② how many times you have been abroad
   ③ how much you like it
   ④ how often you use it

You ordered some tea on the Internet and have received an e-mail from the tea company in London.

Subject:	About your order
Date:	October 12
From:	David Moore (British Tea in London)
To:	Marie Saito

Dear Marie Saito,

Thank you for ordering. Unfortunately, we can sell the orange tea you ordered online only in the U.K. Instead, we can send lemon tea to your country. Its taste and fragrance are as good as those of the orange tea, and we believe you will like it. Would you like us to send it to you, or would you like to cancel your order?

If you want to order it, when do you need it by? We can make sure that you will receive it by any date you specify after October 24th. Also, we need to know how much tea you need. Please let us know these things by e-mail.

Kind regards,
David Moore
Customer services
www.britishteainlondon.co.uk

(138 words)

Questions （目標１分30秒）

1. What did Marie order? ☐ 1 ☐
   ① Black tea.
   ② British tea.
   ③ Lemon tea.
   ④ Orange tea.

2. What did David suggest to Marie? ☐ 2 ☐
   ① He suggested that he could replace the tea she had received with a different one.
   ② He suggested that he could send a different kind of tea.
   ③ He suggested that she should contact the company as soon as possible.
   ④ He suggested that she should make a phone call to the company.

3. David wants Marie to ☐ 3 ☐.
   ① decide what she wants to do about her order
   ② prefer lemon tea to orange tea
   ③ tell him about the amount of the orange tea
   ④ tell him about the date of her order

Lesson 5

対応試験

CEFR A2
共通テスト第１問Ｂ

目標３分10秒　(75 wpm)
237語÷ ☐ 秒×60＝ ☐ wpm
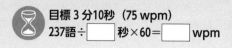

You are going to see a movie on Wednesday, May 1.　You are looking at the theater website.

The 7th Avenue Theater　Contact: XXX-XXXX　🔍 Search　≡

MOVIE TIMES & TICKETS

This page is for finding the best dates and times for you to see the movie.

What's New

A new movie titled "Fantastic Phoenix" will start on May 1.

Ticket Finder

On the following calendar, you can check the dates and times of the movies.　The number in each box shows the percentage of seat tickets that have already been sold in advance.　If the face icon is shown, it means all tickets have been sold, and no seats are available for that showtime.　By clicking each showtime, you can proceed to the purchase page.　Then, decide the number of tickets you need and choose your seats.　If you visit our theater without an advance ticket, you may have to wait in line to buy your movie tickets.

Select Date

Today	Wed.	Thu.	Fri.	Sat.	Sun.
APR 30	MAY 01	MAY 02	MAY 03	MAY 04	MAY 05

Click a movie time to buy your tickets

Strange Adventure　1 hour 33 mins / Fantasy

10:15 a.m.	1:00 p.m.	5:00 p.m.	7:00 p.m.
😫	48%	62%	70%

Dinosaurs　2 hours 2 mins / Documentary

9:30 a.m.	2:00 p.m.	6:00 p.m.
😫	70%	23%

Fantastic Phoenix　3 hours 20 mins / Action　NEW!

10:15 a.m.	2:30 p.m.	6:00 p.m.	10:30 p.m.
95%	😫	95%	82%

The movies which end after 9:00 p.m. (night shows) are only for adults aged 18 or older.

(237 words)

Class	No.	Name

Active
Practical Reading 基本編

Questions (目標 1 分30秒)

1. If the face icon is shown, [1].

   ① it means that you are not old enough to see the movie

   ② no seats are available for that showtime

   ③ the movie will not be shown at that showtime

   ④ you find information about the showtimes of movies

2. If you go to the theater at 2:00 p.m. on May 1 without an advance ticket, you [2].

   ① can enjoy "Fantastic Phoenix" 30 minutes later

   ② have to pay additional money to see any movies

   ③ have to show your ID card to see "Fantastic Phoenix"

   ④ have to wait until 5:00 p.m. to see "Strange Adventure"

3. If you are 16 years old, you can buy an advance ticket for [3].

   ① the 9:30 a.m. showtime of "Dinosaurs"

   ② the 2:30 p.m. showtime of "Fantastic Phoenix"

   ③ the 6:00 p.m. showtime of "Fantastic Phoenix"

   ④ the 7:00 p.m. showtime of "Strange Adventure"

Lesson

6

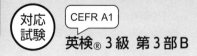
対応試験
英検® 3級 第3部B

CEFR A1

目標 2 分35秒 （78 wpm）
200語÷ ☐ 秒×60＝ ☐ wpm

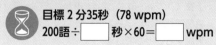

From: Robert Inaba
To: Frank Johnson
Date: November 23
Subject: Flight Information

5 Dear Frank,

How are you? I'm looking forward to staying with you in California during my winter vacation. Could you do me a favor? My plane arrives in Los Angeles at 6:30 a.m. local time. Could you pick me up at the airport? The flight number is AL 178. It is a 10-hour flight from Osaka, Japan.

10 Robert

From: Frank Johnson
To: Robert Inaba
Date: November 24
Subject: Welcome!

15 Hi, Robert.

No problem! I'm looking forward to seeing you, too. I will pick you up at 9:30 a.m. It takes about three hours from my house to the airport by car. Will that be OK? There is a nice café on the 1st floor of the airport. You can relax there until I get there.

20 Frank

From: Robert Inaba
To: Frank Johnson
Date: November 24
Subject: Thank you

25 Thank you, Frank! I like coffee very much! I'll spend some time drinking coffee and reading some books. Coffee will be good for waking me up. 6:30 a.m. in Los Angeles is 11:30 p.m. in my country, Japan. That is a big difference! Looking forward to seeing you soon.

Robert

(200 words)

Class No. Name

Active
Practical Reading 基本編

Questions （目標2分）

1. What is Robert going to do during his winter vacation? [1]
   - ① He will make some coffee for Frank.
   - ② He will pick up Frank at the airport.
   - ③ He will send some information about his flight.
   - ④ He will visit Frank in California.

2. At about what time will Frank leave his home to pick Robert up? [2]
   - ① At about 6:30 a.m.
   - ② At about 9:30 a.m.
   - ③ At about 10:30 p.m.
   - ④ At about 11:30 p.m.

3. What will Robert do after arriving at the airport? [3]
   - ① He will have some coffee and read some books.
   - ② He will kill time in a café until the bus comes.
   - ③ He will rent a car and drive to his friend's house.
   - ④ He will try to wake up at 1:00 a.m. in the morning.

4. At what time in Japan does flight AL 178 leave Osaka? [4]
   - ① At 1:30 p.m. Japan time.
   - ② At 3:30 a.m. Japan time.
   - ③ At 8:30 p.m. Japan time.
   - ④ At 9:30 a.m. Japan time.

Lesson

7

対応試験

CEFR A2

共通テスト第1問B

目標 2 分50秒 (78 wpm)
220語÷□ 秒×60=□ wpm

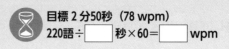

You visited an English website and found an interesting notice.

Call for Student Volunteers: Meeting for Group Discussion Program

We will be holding the annual meeting for our Group Discussion Program. One hundred participants from Japan will visit our city, Vancouver, next August, in order to join in our program. It will be their first visit to Canada. In addition to the Japanese participants, we will have a lot of guests from other countries as well, such as the U.S., Mexico and South Africa.

We are looking for student volunteers to help us with the meeting. We need 10 staff members to show the Japanese participants and the guests around our city, and 25 staff members to manage the event.

Program Schedule

August 4th	Orientation and welcome party
August 5th	Group discussion, part 1: "Global Warming"
August 6th	Presentations on global warming
August 7th	Group discussion, part 2: "Global Economy"
August 8th	Presentations on the global economy
August 9th	Sightseeing in four-country mixed groups with volunteers
August 10th	Farewell party

●Discussions and presentations will be held at the Conference Center.

●The Japanese visitors and some of the other guests are non-native speakers of English, but they have basic English-language skills.

To apply to be a student volunteer, please fill out the **application form** (you can download it from here) and send it to us by Monday, June 20th.

(220 words)

Questions （目標 2 分）

1. The purpose of this notice is to find ☐ 1 ☐ .
   ① foreign volunteers to show the Japanese students around Vancouver
   ② Japanese guests to participate in the group discussion
   ③ student volunteers to help in holding the discussion program
   ④ workers from other countries to help with the event

2. During the meeting, the Japanese participants will ☐ 2 ☐ .
   ① have an opportunity to take English lessons
   ② have discussions about global issues
   ③ have time to travel around Vancouver every day
   ④ make presentations about their own culture

3. The meeting offers a good communication opportunity to the participants and the
   guests because ☐ 3 ☐ .
   ① they will go sightseeing together at the end of the program
   ② they will have discussions in English for the first time
   ③ they will spend most of their time preparing for the discussions
   ④ they will stay in the same accommodations together

4. If you want to be a student volunteer, you should ☐ 4 ☐ .
   ① first download the application form from the website
   ② make a phone call to the office by Monday, June 20th
   ③ prepare a presentation on something you're interested in
   ④ visit the conference center and talk to a staff member

Lesson 8

対応試験

CEFR A2
共通テスト第1問B

目標2分50秒 (82 wpm)
237語÷□秒×60=□wpm

You are visiting a university during its "open campus" day.　You have found a poster about an interesting event.

Starry Light Summer Session

University Professors Meet High School Students

What is the Starry Light Summer Session?

The Starry Light Summer Session (SLSS) is run by the student government of our university.　The purpose of this event is to offer high school students an opportunity to meet university professors and learn more about what is taught at this university.　SLSS welcomes students of all ages.

Date: July 24 from 9:00 a.m. until 5:30 p.m.

Place: The Conference Room

Event: Three professors talk about their own research fields.　See the table below for outlines of the lectures.

Speaker	Research Field	Title and Contents of Lecture
Masa Saito	Agriculture	・How Agriculture Is Affected by Climate Change Three factors important for agriculture —— soil, water and air —— are seriously affected by climate change.
Yoko Collins	Language and Culture	・Language Extinction What is lost when languages die?　Half the languages spoken now will become extinct in the next 100 years.
Linda Adams	Tourism	・Tourism Tourism is one of the most important industries in our prefecture.　Our university is the best place to learn about the business of tourism.

A Challenge for You: Give a Presentation!

We are looking for high school students who are willing to give presentations as part of the lectures listed in the table above.　You will have five minutes to give a presentation in English.　Please prepare slides with photos.　There is more information on our website: https://www.union-slss.org/

(237 words)

Questions （目標2分）

1. SLSS is managed by ___1___ .

   ① high school students

   ② international students

   ③ the student government of the university

   ④ university professors

2. You can learn from the table ___2___ .

   ① how the presentations by professors will be made

   ② what the professors will talk about in their lectures

   ③ when the speakers will make their presentations

   ④ where the specialists have studied their fields

3. Yoko Collins will talk about ___3___ .

   ① climate change and agriculture

   ② language skills with communication devices like slides with photos

   ③ the business of the tourism industry

   ④ what may happen when a language disappears

4. Students who will make presentations in the lectures should ___4___ .

   ① ask the audience a lot of questions

   ② make at least five slides with photos

   ③ speak in English, using slides

   ④ take five minutes to answer questions

You are going to make a pizza for your father.　On a website, you have found a recipe for a pizza that looks delicious.

AN EASY HOMEMADE PIZZA RECIPE

Here is a homemade pizza recipe.　Make perfect pizzas at home in a very quick and easy way with these step-by-step instructions!

Pizza Margherita

Ingredients for two pizzas 25cm in diameter, for about four people：

<u>Pizza dough</u>　　cup ×1 water　　cup ×2 bread flour　　tbsp ×2 olive oil

tsp ×2 baking powder　　tsp ×2 salt　　tsp ×1 sugar

*cup =a cup (200ml),　tbsp =a tablespoon (15ml),　tsp =a teaspoon (5ml)

<u>Toppings</u>　　100ml tomato sauce　　　　fresh basil leaves

50g mozzarella cheese　　　black pepper

Instructions：

<u>Step 1：Make the dough</u>

1. Put the bread flour and baking powder into a large bowl.

2. Pour the water in and stir.

3. Add the olive oil, salt and sugar, and stir until everything is completely mixed.

4. Divide the dough into two balls.

5. Make each ball of dough flat.　Stretch it until it reaches about 25cm across.

<u>Step 2：Bake the pizza with sauce and toppings</u>

1. Spread the sauce and toppings on each pizza.

2. Put the pizzas into the oven and bake for about 10 minutes, until they turn brown.

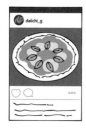

daiichi_g

　　If you use this recipe, why don't you take pictures of your pizzas and post them on your SNS?　We'd love to see your pizza photos!

(201 words)

Class　　No.　　Name

Active
Practical Reading 基本編

Questions （目標2分）

1. This recipe would be good if you want to [1].

　① cook fish for dinner

　② eat something hot and spicy

　③ make pizzas at home quickly and easily

　④ open a pizza restaurant by yourself

2. If you follow the instructions, you will make [2].

　① a 25cm pizza for your parents

　② a pizza with a lot of cheese and onions

　③ twenty-five kinds of pizzas

　④ two pizzas for four people

3. Someone who wants to make pizzas with this recipe needs [3].

　① a liter of water to drink

　② a pot large enough to boil vegetables

　③ an oven large enough to bake pizzas

　④ an SNS account to upload photos to

4. One **opinion** about this recipe is that [4].

　① it is a good idea to post photos of your pizzas on your SNS

　② it is fun to cook with friends

　③ some baking powder is necessary for this recipe

　④ you can find this recipe on the Internet

Lesson
10

対応試験

CEFR A1

共通テスト第2問A

目標2分25秒 (82 wpm)
198語÷□秒×60=□ wpm

As the student in charge of a high school English speech contest in Hyogo prefecture, you are examining all the scores and the comments from three judges to explain the rankings.

Judges' final average scores				
Qualities \ Contestants	Pronunciation (5.0)	Non-verbal communication (5.0)	Content (5.0)	Total (15.0)
Yosuke Nomura	4.2	4.1	4.6	12.9
Rei Matsumoto	4.2	4.0	4.3	12.5
Satsuki Miyazaki	4.6	4.0	4.3	12.9
Kokomi Inaba	4.2	4.0	4.7	12.9

Judges' individual comments	
Ms. Rose	Yosuke's speech was truly informative and thought-provoking. His main topic was one of his personal experiences. However, since he didn't make good eye-contact with his audience, his story did not seem to have been received as he expected.
Mr. Green	I like Satsuki's speech very much! Her speech was fluent and sounded really natural. Not only that, her story was really unique and most of the audience found it interesting.
Ms. Levin	Kokomi's speech was just beautiful in every way. Her pronunciation was almost perfect! She should enter the national speech contest for high school students this year. Regarding Rei's speech, he should have prepared more before the contest.

Judges'shared evaluation (summarized by Ms. Rose)
It was difficult to determine the first, second and third places, because Yosuke, Satsuki, and Kokomi got the same score. We, the judges, have agreed that the pronunciation of the speech is more important than the content because good pronunciation makes the speech clearer and more understandable. Also, we think the content is more important than non-verbal communication.

(198 words)

Questions （目標2分）

1. Based on the judges' final average scores, whose pronunciation was the best?
   1
   ① Yosuke Nomura's was.
   ② Rei Matsumoto's was.
   ③ Satsuki Miyazaki's was.
   ④ Kokomi Inaba's was.

2. Who gave both positive and critical comments? 2
   ① Ms. Rose did.
   ② Mr. Green and Ms. Rose did.
   ③ Ms. Levin did.
   ④ Ms. Rose and Ms. Levin did.

3. One **opinion** from the judges' individual comments and shared evaluation is that
   3 .
   ① a speech becomes easier to understand when it is delivered with good pronunciation
   ② Yosuke's speech was based mostly on his personal experience
   ③ Kokomi's speech received the highest evaluation in terms of content
   ④ Mr. Green praised Satsuki's speech

4. Which of the following is the final ranking based on the judges' shared evaluation?
   4

	1st	2nd	3rd	4th
①	Kokomi Inaba	Yosuke Nomura	Satsuki Miyazaki	Rei Matsumoto
②	Kokomi Inaba	Yosuke Nomura	Rei Matsumoto	Satsuki Miyazaki
③	Kokomi Inaba	Satsuki Miyazaki	Yosuke Nomura	Rei Matsumoto
④	Satsuki Miyazaki	Kokomi Inaba	Yosuke Nomura	Rei Matsumoto
⑤	Satsuki Miyazaki	Kokomi Inaba	Rei Matsumoto	Yosuke Nomura
⑥	Satsuki Miyazaki	Yosuke Nomura	Rei Matsumoto	Kokomi Inaba

スピーキング・トレーナー

本文を音読しよう ☐   179語÷[   ]秒×60=[   ]wpm

You are going to have a debate about learning a foreign language at school. You've found an interesting blog post.

Learning Another Language at School

High schools in Japan require their students to learn another language, such as
5   English. A recent survey shows that learning a foreign language helps the learners see things from different angles. Also, according to several studies in the U.S., English-speakers who learn a second language have better listening skills and greater understanding of their native language.

> **Tim@Tim0104**
> I think that students have good opportunities to learn other cultures and
10   values by learning a foreign language. They understand the importance of respecting people with different values. When traveling to another country, students can communicate with the local people in their native language, as well.
> 15   2021.1.16

Others believe that schools should not make the students study another language.

> **Chloe@life_design_C**
> Learning a foreign language may be too difficult for some students.
> Each language has its own rules, sounds and letters. Learning them
> 20   is not easy at all. Also, knowing a foreign language is not useful for some students. If they do not go to other countries, they may never use the language.
> 2021.1.30

What do you think? In my view, learning another language at school is necessary
25   in order to survive in this highly globalized world. Research suggests that more than half the world's people can speak two or more languages.

(211 words)

Questions（目標 2 分）

1. One **fact** from the blog post is that ☐ 1 ☐.
   ① learning a foreign language is a good opportunity to experience another culture
   ② learning a foreign language is not easy because each language has its own rules
   ③ a person's ability in a second language has positive effects on that person's listening skills in his or her native language
   ④ we need foreign language skills to survive in this highly globalized world

2. You want to collect opinions **supporting** the idea of learning another language at school.　One such opinion in the blog post is that students ☐ 2 ☐.
   ① can improve their physical and mental health
   ② mostly have studied foreign languages before
   ③ will have opportunities to learn other cultures and values
   ④ will learn how to speak another language fluently

3. Which of the following pieces of information would you need to make Chloe's opinion more persuasive? ☐ 3 ☐
   ① A survey on people's attitudes toward different cultures and values.
   ② A survey on reasons why foreign languages are difficult to learn.
   ③ The average time a Japanese baby needs to learn his or her native language.
   ④ The percentage of Japanese people who don't want to learn English.

4. The writer of this blog post ☐ 4 ☐ the idea of learning another language at school.
   ① basically has a negative attitude toward
   ② does not have any particular opinion about
   ③ strongly agrees with
   ④ strongly disagrees with

Lesson 12

対応試験

CEFR A2

GTEC® パートC
英検®準2級 第4部B

目標2分20秒 (90 wpm)
212語÷ [　] 秒×60= [　] wpm

Most of us tend to think that blue is for boys and pink is for girls. According to an article in the early 1900s, however, pink was for boys and blue was for girls. The reason is that pink was seen as a strong color and blue was seen as a delicate color.

From the 1940s, people tried to change this situation. They started to think that girls should be as strong as boys and boys should be more kind to others. This idea was introduced into choosing colors. More girls started to choose pink and more boys started to choose blue. Even in a toy store, there were a blue section and a pink section. The blue section was mainly for boys and it had toy cars and building blocks. The pink section was mainly for girls and it was full of dolls and cooking toys.

Now, many people think this situation should change. Some toy stores in Europe and the U.S. no longer separate toys into a boys' section and a girls' section. They feel that children should freely choose what they want to play with and learn a lot of things from it. This will help us make a better world for both boys and girls in the future.

(212 words)

Class　　No.　　Name

Questions （目標2分）

1. Pink was once thought of as $\boxed{\quad 1 \quad}$.

　① a delicate color for boys

　② a delicate color for girls

　③ a strong color for boys

　④ a strong color for girls

2. From the 1940s, people started to think that $\boxed{\quad 2 \quad}$.

　① boys have to wear blue clothes

　② boys should be stronger than girls

　③ girls don't have to be less strong than boys

　④ girls should behave more kindly than boys

3. In toy stores, $\boxed{\quad 3 \quad}$.

　① dolls and cooking toys were found in a blue section

　② there was a blue section mainly for girls

　③ there were separate sections for boys and for girls

　④ toy cars and building blocks were found in a pink section

4. Why do some toy stores no longer have boys' and girls' sections? $\boxed{\quad 4 \quad}$

　① Because they do not like pink and blue colors.

　② Because they do not think children should choose what they want.

　③ Because they suggest children should buy more toys.

　④ Because they think all toys are for all children.

Lesson

13

対応試験

CEFR A1

共通テスト第2問A

目標 2分35秒 （90 wpm）
230語÷ ☐ 秒×60= ☐ wpm

You would like to build a bookshelf by yourself.　You are looking at the instructions for your bookshelf.

WOLF Bookshelf: How to Assemble It

The "WOLF" model is a basic bookshelf kit.　It has a wide variety of sizes and colors.　It is easy to use this kit, so we can strongly recommend it to beginners.

Step 1: Check the parts

back panel ×1	side panel ×2	top [bottom] board ×2
shelf board ×2	wood dowel ×8	nail ×4　　metal pin ×8

Step 2: Build the frame

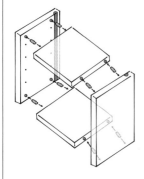

Put four of the wood dowels into the holes of one side panel. Two of the dowels are used for the bottom board and the other two are for the top board.　Carefully put the bottom board and the top board onto the dowels in the side panel. Put the other four wood dowels into the holes of the other side panel.　Then, carefully place the side panel on the two boards you have already put up.

Step 3: Attach the back panel

Put the back panel between the side panels and slide it down from the top.　Then, use a hammer to put two nails into the top board and two nails into the bottom board to fix the back panel.

Step 4: Insert the middle shelf boards

Stand up the bookshelf and put in the eight metal pins to hold up the two middle shelves.　You can move them to other holes to put the shelves at different heights.

(230 words)

Class　　No.　　Name

Active
Practical Reading 基本編

Questions （目標2分）

1. These instructions will be helpful if you ☐ **1** ☐ .
   ① do not know how to make a bookshelf
   ② have a nice tool kit to build a shelf
   ③ need help from a carpenter
   ④ want to order a bookshelf online

2. If you want to build this bookshelf, you ☐ **2** ☐ .
   ① do not need any tools
   ② have to buy an electric drill
   ③ should work with at least two other people
   ④ will need a hammer

3. If you follow the instructions, you will get a bookshelf ☐ **3** ☐ .
   ① in which you can change the height of the middle shelves
   ② which has seven shelves
   ③ which is easy to put together and take apart
   ④ which is made of steel

4. One **opinion** stated in these instructions is that ☐ **4** ☐ .
   ① the nails are for attaching the back panel to the top and bottom shelves
   ② the wood dowels are mainly used for side panels
   ③ this bookshelf is good for beginners
   ④ you can put the two middle shelves at different heights

When you were preparing for the debate in the next English class, you found an interesting article on a website.

School Rules in Japan

By Sarah Willy, London
14 January 2016 5:18 PM

When I first visited a high school in Osaka, Japan, I found a lot of surprising rules that the students must follow at their school.   Here are some of them.

1. Students must wear their uniforms every day.   They cannot attend school without their uniforms.   This includes school shoes and neckties.
2. Students should not change their natural appearance, for example, dyeing their hair, wearing makeup, or wearing colored contacts.
3. Students should not wear a bright-colored sweater or jacket during winter.   They may only wear a navy or black sweater or jacket.
4. Students should not use their mobile phones while they are in the school building.
5. Students must be at school by 8:35 a.m.   If a student is late five times, he or she must do some cleaning after school.

When I saw some high school students in Japan, I felt that they looked too young for their age.   It seems that Japanese students are used to following rules, but they are not used to judging what is wrong and what is right by themselves.   Therefore, at least to me, it seems that they are educated to fit into Japanese society through their unique school rules.

18 Comments
Newest

Alastair   19 February 2016   8:11 PM
Rules are necessary when children are growing up.   If they do not have any opportunity to learn why they should obey school rules, they won't know the importance of obeying laws after growing up.

(254 words)

Class   No.   Name

Active
Practical Reading 基本編

Questions （目標 2 分）

1. According to the rules explained in the article, students in a high school in Osaka are not allowed to ☐ 1 ☐.
   ① do cleaning after school
   ② dye their hair and wear makeup
   ③ use their mobile phones while they are at home
   ④ wear a navy jacket

2. In the 2nd paragraph of the article, "they looked too young for their age" means that ☐ 2 ☐.
   ① they didn't look as mature as students of the same age in the writer's country
   ② they have been really young for a long time
   ③ they were so young that they could not grow up
   ④ they were too young to enter school

3. Your team will support the opinion "School rules are necessary" in a debate.　In the article, one **opinion** helpful for your team is that ☐ 3 ☐.
   ① students are used to judging what is right and what is wrong
   ② students have to wear their school uniforms
   ③ students learn the importance of following rules from school rules
   ④ students should not use their mobile phones

4. Judging his comment, Alastair ☐ 4 ☐ the school rules stated in the article.
   ① does not agree with
   ② does not have any positive opinions about
   ③ seems to agree with
   ④ seems to have different opinions about

Lesson 15

対応試験

CEFR A2
英検®準2級 第4部A

目標 2分35秒 （90 wpm）
236語÷□秒×60=□wpm

From: Barry Gallagher <barryg.114@ymail.com>
To: Diana Gallagher <d-gallagher84@ymail.com>
Date: January 14
Subject: About "Career Day"

5　Hi, Aunt Diana,

How are you doing?　I was happy seeing you last weekend at my grandparents' house for Sunday lunch.　I didn't know my grandpa is such a good cook!　I loved the roast beef that he cooked for us.　Also, the chocolate cake you brought for us was really nice as well.　I would like to know where you bought it.

10　Can I ask you a favor?　Next month, we are going to have "Career Day" at my high school.　On that day, we learn about different careers, so our teachers are looking for some people who can talk about their jobs.

I heard from my mother that you have been an architect for more than 20 years. Would you come to our school and talk about your job in front of the students?　We
15　are really interested in your career.　I strongly believe that your experience will be helpful for us in deciding what job we should take.

Career Day will be held in the school hall.　We will invite a lot of guest speakers. They are an editor, a doctor, a programmer, a lawyer, a bank teller, and a hair stylist. All of them will make a speech for the students about their own job, too.　If you can
20　help us, please let me know.
Best,
Barry

(236 words)

Class　　No.　　Name

Questions （目標2分）

1. On the last weekend, _____1_____ .
   ① Barry had dinner with his family
   ② Barry's grandfather finally became a professional chef
   ③ Barry's grandmother baked a cheesecake for her family
   ④ Diana took a chocolate cake to her parents' house

2. What will Barry do next month? ___2___
   ① He will cook roast beef at his school.
   ② He will meet his elementary school teachers.
   ③ He will start a new job at his school.
   ④ He will take part in a school event.

3. Barry asks Diana to ___3___ .
   ① come to school and help the students get their jobs
   ② go to her old school and tell the teachers what she does now
   ③ take him to school and have a chat with his homeroom teacher
   ④ visit his school and talk about what she does for work

4. The students at Barry's school can ___4___ .
   ① get little information about how to become a doctor
   ② invite a lot of guests and make a speech about them
   ③ listen to talks from people with various jobs
   ④ make a presentation in front of editors, doctors, or programmers

Lesson
16

対応試験

CEFR A1
共通テスト第3問A

目標2分45秒 (95 wpm)
261語÷ □ 秒×60= □ wpm

Your Australian friend Jessica visited a Japanese summer festival and wrote an article about her experience on the Internet.

A Japanese Summer Festival

Wednesday, August 3

In Japan, it is summer now.   The other day, my friend Mariko took me to a Japanese summer festival.   I had never been to a Japanese festival before.

There were a lot of food stands there.   I first tried *yakisoba*, which was Japanese fried noodles.   It had a lot of meat and vegetables in it, and it was seasoned with a salty-sweet sauce.   Then we found an interesting carnival game.   Surprisingly, people were trying to catch living goldfish!   They were scooping up goldfish, and it was called *kingyo-sukui* in Japanese.   I tried it once, but I couldn't get any goldfish at all.   They were moving around too quickly!

After that, we saw people doing a dance called *bon-odori*.   A lot of kids were enjoying dancing to traditional Japanese music.   They danced well and they looked like they were having fun.   Mariko invited me to join in the dance and I really wanted to, but I hesitated to do so because I didn't know how to dance.

By the time the people finished their dance, it had become dark.   Mariko told me that fireworks were going to start soon.   Before finding a good place to see the fireworks, I bought a candied apple at the stand between the goldfish-scooping stand and the cotton-candy stand.   When I saw the fireworks, I was impressed that they were so much more beautiful than I had expected.

I enjoyed that great summer festival with beautiful fireworks, stands and games. It was really nice to experience such unique Japanese traditions.

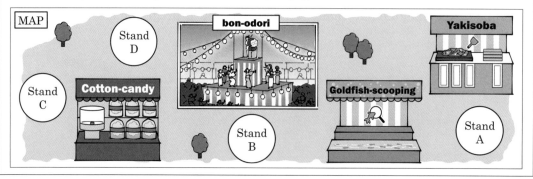

(261 words)

Class   No.   Name

Active
Practical Reading 基本編

Questions （目標2分）

1. According to this article, the writer ☐ 1 ☐.
   ① ate *yakisoba*, which one of her friends had cooked
   ② wanted to go to a Japanese festival but couldn't
   ③ was familiar with Japanese festivals
   ④ went to a Japanese festival for the first time

2. The writer enjoyed ☐ 2 ☐.
   ① doing a Japanese dance
   ② doing shooting games
   ③ having ramen noodles
   ④ watching Japanese fireworks

3. At which stand did the writer buy a candied apple? ☐ 3 ☐.
   ① Stand A
   ② Stand B
   ③ Stand C
   ④ Stand D

4. From this article, we know that the writer ☐ 4 ☐.
   ① didn't think that Japanese fireworks were so beautiful
   ② had a good time at the Japanese summer festival
   ③ joined in *bon-odori* and enjoyed it very much
   ④ took Mariko to a Japanese summer festival

Lesson

17

対応試験

CEFR A1

共通テスト第3問A

目標2分35秒 (95 wpm)
247語÷ □ 秒×60= □ wpm

You want to visit a country called Rakouzhia and you have found the following blog post.

My Summer Holiday on Melony Island

Sunday, June 5

5 I went with my husband to a country named Rakouzhia for our honeymoon and we visited Melony Island, which is located to the north of the mainland of Rakouzhia. Melony Island is joined to the mainland by a train bridge, so we took the train from Tatsuma City to get to the island.   The scenery from the train on the bridge was beautiful and I felt as if we were floating on the sea.

10 We were planning to enjoy surfing, but unfortunately, the beach was crowded with other tourists.   So we gave up enjoying ourselves on the beach and went to our hotel instead.   We took a hot spring bath in the hotel.   In the evening, we enjoyed a steak dinner.   It was so tasty!

The next morning, we enjoyed surfing on the beach near our hotel.   In the
15 afternoon, we went to a local café and enjoyed coffee and sweets.   In the evening, we went to a restaurant on the top of a mountain.   We enjoyed seeing a beautiful sunset and stars over dinner.

On the last day, we rented a car and went to many famous places around the island.   We visited scenic spots, temples and gift shops.   We didn't get lost when
20 driving around the island because the hotel staff had given us a detailed map of the island.

We spent a great holiday there.   I really want to go to the island again someday.

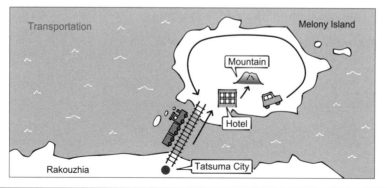

(247 words)

Class   No.   Name

Questions（目標 2 分）

1. The couple went to Rakouzhia to 　1　 .
   ① build a train bridge which would join Melony Island to the mainland
   ② celebrate the 10th anniversary of their marriage
   ③ have a vacation after their wedding
   ④ visit their parents and relatives living there

2. The couple went to Melony Island from 　2　 .
   ① Tatsuma City by car
   ② Tatsuma City by train
   ③ their hotel by car
   ④ their hotel by train

3. What did the couple do on Melony Island? 　3　
   ① They enjoyed a shared bus tour on the last day.
   ② They enjoyed themselves at a hot spring in the hotel.
   ③ They went surfing on the day when they arrived at Melony Island.
   ④ They went to a restaurant on the mountain and enjoyed lunch.

4. From this blog post, you have learned that 　4　 .
   ① there are a lot of famous places on Melony Island to visit by car
   ② visiting Melony Island in June is the best choice because it is warmer then
   ③ you can enjoy surfing even if there are a lot of people
   ④ you can enjoy various kinds of food at reasonable prices

Lesson
18

対応試験

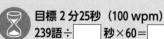

CEFR A2
GTEC® パートC
英検®準2級 第4部B

目標2分25秒（100 wpm）
239語÷ ___ 秒×60＝ ___ wpm

Twins

What do we call people who have a brother or sister who was born on the same day as them? We call them twins.

We scientists have long had an interest in twins as a subject of our research. When I
5 taught two pairs of twins at college ten years ago, I asked them how they spent their time together. Each twin answered the questions separately. Both pairs said they stayed together almost all the time and did the same activities at the same time—studying, watching TV, and so on. When I asked them what subjects they liked, one pair's favorite subjects were all the same. The other pair had three subjects in
10 common. Finally, I asked them to talk about their own personality. Surprisingly, each twin said almost the same thing! That was the most interesting thing to me.

Sometimes twins move apart immediately after they are born. Even in such cases, they sometimes do the same things. For example, one pair of twins met each other 40 years after they were separated, and to their surprise, the twins found that their wives
15 had the same name. In addition, their children were born on the same day and had the same name.

Twins share characteristics of their parents with each other. If there are any differences between them, where do the differences come from? We expect that something new will be found by studying twins further.

(239 words)

Class   No.   Name

Questions （目標 2 分）

1. The writer was 　1　.
   ① a science teacher at a high school
   ② a teacher of a lot of twins
   ③ a teacher of two pairs of twins at college
   ④ asked some questions by twins

2. The writer found that 　2　.
   ① all pairs of twins like the same subjects at school
   ② twins are likely to choose the same job and work at the same office
   ③ twins are most interested in their personalities
   ④ twins seem to have similar personalities

3. The writer says twins sometimes 　3　.
   ① do the same things even when they have not seen each other for a long time
   ② give their children the same names when they live together
   ③ have the same name because their parents like it very much
   ④ keep in touch with each other even when they live in different places

4. Which of the following is true about the scientists mentioned in this passage?
   　4　
   ① They are going to study more about twins to find out something new.
   ② They are interested in twins and they like to teach twins at school.
   ③ They found that not all pairs of twins share the same characteristics as their parents.
   ④ They have found out all the differences between twins.

You have found the following article in a tourist magazine.

How to Enjoy Japanese Food
Eric Martin

Japanese food is no longer only for Japanese people.　It has become popular all over the world.　A lot of people are familiar with typical Japanese foods, such as sushi and tempura.　You have probably had Japanese foods in your own country, haven't you?　However, do you know how to enjoy Japanese foods properly?　Some people are not sure about how to eat them.

When you enter a restaurant in Japan, a server will offer you a wet towel or a wet napkin.　You use it to wipe your hands.　If it is given to you on a bamboo or plastic tray, please put it back on the tray after you've wiped your hands so that you can use it again whenever you need to.

It is rude to make noises while eating in the U.S.　However, in Japan, the situation is different.　When you eat Japanese noodles, such as *soba* and ramen, it's OK to make a slurping noise.　You may be surprised to know that you should make a sipping sound when you drink a cup of green tea at the end of a tea ceremony to show you are content with the ceremony.　If you are not used to making some noise while eating or drinking, you should practice it!

Finally, I would like to tell you how to use chopsticks.　Please avoid holding food with two pairs of chopsticks.　That is believed to bring bad luck.　If you want to pass food to another person, put it on a plate first so that the person can take it with his or her own chopsticks.

I hope this article will be helpful to you when you go to Japan.　Enjoy Japan's food and its culture!

(295 words)

Class　　No.　　Name

Questions (目標2分)

1. The writer writes about Japanese food manners in the following order: $\boxed{\quad 1 \quad}$.
   ① using a wet towel → drinking green tea at a tea ceremony → eating Japanese noodles → using chopsticks
   ② using a wet towel → eating Japanese noodles → using chopsticks → drinking green tea at a tea ceremony
   ③ using a wet towel → eating Japanese noodles → drinking green tea at a tea ceremony → using chopsticks
   ④ using a wet towel → using chopsticks → eating Japanese noodles → drinking green tea at a tea ceremony

2. Many people around the world already know much about $\boxed{\quad 2 \quad}$.
   ① a bamboo or plastic tray
   ② how to eat Japanese foods
   ③ some typical Japanese dishes
   ④ the Japanese tea ceremony

3. If you do not make a noise while drinking tea at the end of a tea ceremony, that may imply that $\boxed{\quad 3 \quad}$.
   ① you are not happy with the ceremony
   ② you are satisfied with the ceremony
   ③ you know a lot about the manners of the ceremony
   ④ you want one more cup of tea

4. From this article, you have learned that $\boxed{\quad 4 \quad}$.
   ① it is rude to make a noise when eating *soba* in Japan
   ② Japanese foods are not popular at all among people in other countries
   ③ you should practice making a noise when eating Japanese noodles
   ④ you should use two pairs of chopsticks when passing food to another person

Today, many of us try to live in a way that will damage the environment as little as possible.　We recycle newspapers and plastic bottles, we take trains or buses to get to work, and we stopped using some products which are bad for our environment years ago.

5　Now, we want to take these ideas to the places that we visit on holidays.　This is called "ecotourism."　It has three main purposes.　First, we protect the wild animals and culture of the area.　Second, we do not damage the natural environment.　Third, we spend money for the local people and help the local community.

One good example of an ecotourism project is making the number of tourists which 10　visit the tourist site at the same time smaller.　By doing so, we make the influence on the natural environment as small as possible.　If too many people visit a place, it may be difficult for the local people to protect the environment.

If you want to enjoy ecotourism, here is some important advice.　First, it may be a good idea to learn about the culture and history of the place that you are going to visit. 15　If you know about them, you will not only see the sights but also feel closer to them. Also, it is important to learn some simple phrases of the native language, like "Thank you." or "Good morning."　If you use them with the local people, they will smile and become friendly toward you.　These ways of enjoying tourism will never harm the environment.

20　Remember the phrase "Leave nothing behind you except footprints and take nothing away except photographs."　Respect the places you visit, just as you respect your own hometown.

(285 words)

Questions （目標2分）

1. According to the passage, how do many of us try to protect our environment?

　　1

　① By recycling, going to work by train, and not using expensive products.

　② By recycling, taking our own car to work, and using things again.

　③ By recycling, taking taxis to work, and using eco-bags.

　④ By recycling, using public transportation, and not using products that are bad for the environment.

2. Which of the following is NOT a purpose of ecotourism given in the passage?

　　2

　① To help the local people and community by spending money there.

　② To protect the animals and culture of the area a tourist visits.

　③ To try not to damage the natural environment.

　④ To try to improve the natural environment by planting trees.

3. A good example of an ecotourism project is 　3　.

　① a lot of tourists trying to protect the environment

　② a lot of tourists visiting a tourist site at the same time

　③ tourists not going to a protected area

　④ tourists visiting a tourist site in a small group

4. What is important in order to enjoy ecotourism? 　4

　① To introduce your hometown to the local people.

　② To leave something valuable for tourists.

　③ To master a foreign language.

　④ To respect the local place.

You found the following story written by a musician in a newspaper.

Music Meets Technology

Steven Marshall

5   After graduating from university in London, I started working as a musician in the 1970s.   I first performed as a professional music player in New York.   Every night, I loved to walk around and search for rare records because there were a lot of famous record shops in New York.   Good music taught me everything I needed as a musician.   I spent twenty years working in New York.

     After that, I moved to Tokyo.   Tokyo was a busy city like New York.   However, 10   one thing that was very different was that technology controlled the city.   That was my first impression of Tokyo.

     Now, in the 21st century, technology has changed the way people listen to music. People do not go to CD shops so often.   Fewer young people buy music CDs. Instead, they download music through the Internet.   This is because most music is 15   sold on the Internet.   If you have digital copies of music in your music player, you can listen to them anytime and anywhere.

     Also, technology has had a great impact on the way music is created.   In the past, musicians had to go to the same studio and play together to record their music.   I recorded music that way with a lot of musicians in the 1970s.   Now, we mainly use 20   computers when composing music.   The other day, I sent my recording data from here in Sydney to other band members in Singapore by e-mail!   Even if we are in different countries, we can still create music together.

     When I was in Tokyo 25 years ago, I thought people around the world, including musicians, would not be able to live without technology.   But I also believed 25   musicians would not be replaced by technology.   Even today, a large audience is waiting for our live music performances!

(304 words)

Questions （目標2分）

1. Choose the four cities in the order the writer of this story lived in them.

   $\boxed{1}$ → $\boxed{2}$ → $\boxed{3}$ → $\boxed{4}$

   ① London

   ② New York

   ③ Singapore

   ④ Sydney

   ⑤ Tokyo

2. The writer says that $\boxed{5}$.

   ① music made by digital technology is much better than older music

   ② people today can live without music

   ③ people today enjoy music only on the Internet

   ④ the way music is created has been changed by technology

3. While the writer was in Tokyo 25 years ago, he $\boxed{6}$.

   ① believed musicians would become less popular

   ② believed technology would not take the place of musicians

   ③ thought musicians should use digital technology in their music

   ④ thought people and technology should not exist together

4. What has been the career of the writer? $\boxed{7}$

   ① He became a professional musician in the 1970s and still plays music.

   ② He lived in Tokyo for ten years and worked as a musician.

   ③ He started his career in London and now lives in Singapore.

   ④ He started to create music on the Internet after he graduated from university.

You found the following article written by a journalist.

Mobile Wallets' Advantages and Disadvantages Sara Brian

Mobile wallets are becoming more and more popular in Japan. They are usually designed to run on mobile devices, such as smartphones. Before starting to use mobile wallets, you should know several advantages and disadvantages they have.

Advantages

1. Mobile wallets make more space in your bag.

   If you are carrying a mobile wallet, you don't need to carry a lot of cards and cash with you when you go out. Using mobile wallets is a good way to have more space in your bag or pocket.

2. They are much safer than normal wallets.

   A wallet is locked by a password. In addition, information about your money or cards is put in your mobile wallet as encrypted data. So your money remains highly secure even if your smartphone is stolen. Mobile wallets are much safer than traditional ones. I think this is their biggest advantage.

3. You can pay faster.

   You can pay faster than you can by taking money out of your traditional wallet. This is because you don't have to count the number of coins in your wallet and salesclerks don't have to give you change.

Disadvantages

1. Mobile wallets need batteries.

   Mobile wallets are on your smartphone. Therefore, if the battery runs out, you cannot use them anymore. You should be careful about this when you depend on your mobile wallet for everyday shopping.

2. You may spend too much money.

   You may not really feel you are spending money when using a mobile wallet. When you want to buy something, you just have to show your smartphone to the salesclerk, so you may possibly spend more money than you think.

No one leaves home without their wallet now. However, mobile wallets will change this situation. Japan is moving toward being a cashless society.

(305 words)

Class   No.   Name

Active
Practical Reading 基本編

Questions （目標2分）

1. Put the following points（①〜⑤）regarding mobile wallets into the order in which they are discussed in the article.　　1 → 2 → 3 → 4 → 5
   ① Dependence on electric power
   ② Possibility of wasting money
   ③ Reduction of luggage
   ④ Security
   ⑤ Speed of transactions

2. The writer says that　6　.
   ① a store clerk gives us change if we pay with our mobile wallet
   ② many people still need to bring many cards while carrying mobile wallets
   ③ the biggest advantage of mobile wallets is their high-level security
   ④ we can take cash out of our mobile wallets

3. A mobile wallet needs a battery　7　.
   ① because it is convenient to use
   ② because it runs on a mobile device
   ③ in order to be used every day
   ④ in order to be used more freely

4. How will mobile wallets change our current situation?　8
   ① We will carry fewer things when going out.
   ② We will go out less frequently to buy things we need.
   ③ We will save a lot more money than we do now.
   ④ We will spend less time using our smartphones.